THE

DISPLACED

CHILDREN

OF

DISPLACED

CHILDREN

JUDGE'S CITATION

Mohyuddin's craft is composed of measurable
touches that go hardly noticed. And the subject! Serious stuff,
yes, but the collection contains a variety of tones and concerns.
There is the jelly-fish in space (lament though the poem may be),
a talking banana, bingeing on pumpkin pie. To be sure, the title
refers to diaspora and the poems refer to families in and immigrants
from Pakistan. There are literal landscapes and clear memories to be
enjoyed. And yet, because these poems are so well crafted and the
emotion so well expressed, the subject matter is overtaken by such
themes as boundary, legacy, loss, claim. Whether a long narrative
poem, or shorter lyric poems, these are the works of a poet
mature in his concerns and thinking.

— Kimiko Hahn, final judge of the 2017 Sexton Prize for Poetry

THE DISPLACED CHILDREN OF DISPLACED CHILDREN

FAISAL MOHYUDDIN

EYEWEAR PUBLISHING

WINNER
The Sexton Prize for Poetry 2017

First published in 2018
by Eyewear Publishing Ltd
Suite 333, 19-21 Crawford Street
Marylebone, London w1h 1pj
United Kingdom

Cover design and typeset by Edwin Smet
Cover image by Wikipedia Commons
Author photograph by Ariel Tesher

Printed in England by TJ International Ltd, Padstow, Cornwall

isbn 978-1-912477-06-7

FSC
MIX
Paper from
responsible sources
www.fsc.org   FSC® C013056

*The editor has generally followed American spelling
and punctuation at the author's request.*

WWW.EYEWEARPUBLISHING.COM

for my mother
Rahat Mohyuddin

&

in memory of my father
Mohammad Mohyuddin
(1944–2015)

Faisal Mohyuddin,
a child of immigrants from Pakistan,
is the author of the chapbook *The Riddle of Longing*
(Backbone Press, 2017). He is the recipient of the
Edward Stanley Award from *Prairie Schooner* and a
Gwendolyn Brooks Poetry Award. A graduate of
Carleton College, Northwestern University, and
Columbia College Chicago, he is also an alumnus of
the US Department of State's Teachers for Global
Classrooms program. He teaches English at Highland
Park High School in Illinois, serves as an educator
adviser to the global not-for-profit Narrative 4,
and lives with his wife and son in Chicago.
The Displaced Children of Displaced Children
is his debut full-length collection.

TABLE OF CONTENTS

IV

A CLOSING

We have come to know our existence can never be erased.
Even though, for centuries, history has been our enemy.

Iqbal, we have no confidante in this troubled world –
So what can anyone ever know of our hidden anguish?

– Allama Iqbal

THE OPENING

THE CHILD: Tell me, Father,
what new turbulence took hold
in your blood on the day of my birth,
and did your stomach sink
each time I cried out for the basket
of your arms?

THE FATHER: I held you too close
to feel anything but the wild
gallop of your tiny heart.

THE CHILD: Did you recite
the call to prayer in my ear, slip
your pinky, dipped in honey, in my mouth
to mark with song and sweetness
my entry into the ummah
of the Prophet Muhammad,
peace be upon him?

THE FATHER: All night, I nursed
a candle's flame, leaning in and out
of its sphere of light, mumbling verses
of the Qur'an, mispronouncing
the Arabic, not understanding a word
beyond 'Al-Fatiha', but knowing,
nonetheless, I had fulfilled
this first obligation of fatherhood.

THE CHILD: What was it like
to look into my eyes for the first time?

THE FATHER: I felt as if my fingers
had combed the embryonic silt feathering
the deepest bottom of the ocean.
And when I resurfaced, holding the key
to fatherhood, I understood
the true worth of being a living thing.

THE CHILD: What did you say
to Mother when she could not find
the words to tell you about how
the breaking open of a body
propels one toward heaven, that God
promises the greatest share of Paradise
to mothers?

THE FATHER: After a long silence,
I said, 'To every unutterable thing
buried in your heart, to every miraculous truth
teetering on the tip of your tongue,
yes, yes, *ameen*'.

THE CHILD: Did you spill the blood
of two goats, give their meat to the poor,
to bless my arrival, to mark
the transition of my soul
from the library of the eternal
into the living fire of a body too fragile to share?

THE FATHER: For twenty years,
I harvested the silhouette of my father's voice
from the night sky, let its echo rock me
to sleep whenever I felt so crushed

by heartache that even God's infinite love,
a rescue vessel sailing through a history
of bloodshed and loss, could not hold me
intact enough to believe in survival –
so if it was my hand or another's
that guided the blade along two throats
I cannot recall, nor do I want to.

THE CHILD: What else
might you have done
had fatherhood not stolen you
from the life you knew?

THE FATHER: When a surgeon
saves your life by amputating a limb
housing a reservoir of poison,
you do not curse the violence
of his work, nor the pain of the procedure.
You bow down before God,
you thank the man, you learn to write
with the other hand, to walk
on one leg.

THE CHILD: One final question,
Father. What should I say
when my son, when I too become a father,
asks me about the hours
of your life that exist beyond
my knowing?

THE FATHER: Tell him more
about the hours of your life
so his hunger is not as desperate
nor as bottomless
as ours.

I

GHAZAL FOR THE DIASPORA

We have always been the displaced children of displaced children,
Tethered by distant rivers to abandoned lands, our blood's history lost.

To temper the grief, imagine your father's last breath as a Moghul garden –
Marble pool at its center, the mirrored sky holding all his tribe had lost.

Above the tussle of his wounded city, sad-eyed paper kites fight to stay aloft.
One lucky child will be crowned the winner, everyone else will have lost.

Wish peace upon every stranger who arrives at your door, even the thief –
For you never know when your last chance at redemption will be lost.

In another version of the story, a steady loneliness mothers away the rust.
Yet, without windows in its hull, the time-traveler's supplication gets lost.

Against flame-lipped testimonies of exile's erasures, the swinging of an axe.
Felled banyan trees populate your nightmares, new enlightenments lost.

The rim of this porcelain cup is chipped, so sip with practiced caution.
Even a trace of blood will copper the flavor, the respite of tea now lost.

Tell me, Faisal, with what new surrender can you evade deeper damnation?
Whatever it is, hack away, before your children too become the Lost.

OF THE PUNJAB

Exile begins where rivers end.

I dream my limbs and head are the five rivers that make fertile
the land of my ancestors. I dream about wild music,
about longing, about an end to thirst.

My tongue ploughs through black silt, lifting scraps
of language, history, myth.

Along the Ravi, Jahangir's molecules have migrated
from his decaying tomb, into the whistling sweetness of water.
I taste the emperor's fishy eyes, his inky breath,
the aching vacancies of his toothless gums. I taste lost time.

Where my father lived as a boy, fatherless,
in a stone house with shuttered windows, a girl now sits,
her face caged by shadows, embroidering with golden thread a bouquet
by candlelight. Held like a thin drum between her knees,
a wood frame holds taut the black silk.

Her needle plunges, resurfaces. Gardenias bloom
in every mohalla of Lahore.

The sputtering moths orbiting the flame
grow giddy on perfumed air, lose their caution, burn.

Behind me, a blind cartographer beckons.
He promises a new empire, my claim upon it brokered by worms
and the wind-borne remnants of lost names.

I claw open a grave at the girl's feet. I recite the alphabet.
I unbraid the water from my blood and surrender to the soil.
I let darkness fall in earthy clumps until I am crushed.

The girl wraps the tombstone with the black cloth,
falls to her knees like a fellow pilgrim. She begins to hum.

I wake to the haunted chatter of rain.

PARTITION, AND THEN

We were looking for _____ we found _____.
– Carolyn Forché

The night is an empty basket, and the long journey ahead
promises to be weighed down by hunger, luminous

and wild. As they cross into the newly-formed nation,
a child, cargo strapped to her mother's back, takes the black

sheet of sky and folds it seven times to make a horse,
then fashions wings for it knitted from thin ribbons of wind.

Inside the brick temple of her mother's grasping heart,
a burning nest of nightjars, their feathers flecked with both

copper's shimmer and its blue decay. Their calls sound like stones
skipping across the surface of a river. Before the new day

tears open the stillness of her reveries, the girl rests her cheek
between her mother's shoulders and rolls herself back into

the womb. Inside, the rivers of the newly broken world
flow backwards toward the Himalayas, returning first to snow,

then to cloud. At the first blue blush of dawn, the child
begins to collect the stars, loses count, begins again, and then

again, until sleep arrives and she becomes a white ember of light,
exiled from her sky. In the distance, blindfolded theologians

straddle the gash drawn by Mountbatten's pen, holding vials
of new blood, large spoons carved from ivory, and honey.

PAKISTAN, FATHERLESS

If Jinnah had lived, his life extending into the summer and autumn of
Pakistan's seasons of growth, seen vision translated into the ordinariness
of reality, while still sustaining its spirit, maybe the country would be in a
different place.
– from Rafia Zakaria in *Dawn*

Possibly it broke his heart – when Jinnah divined,

As he recognized, in half-sleep, the Angel of Death

Kneeling at the foot of his bed, softly reciting

Iqbal's 'Taranah-e-Hindi', that neither supplication nor

Streptomycin would save him, that his second child,

The nation itself, would by nightfall become

Another orphan left forever to pine for her father,

Nursed not by his own hand, but its ineffectual shadow.

SONG

My father is in the kitchen
making a morning
cup of tea, singing a song
he first heard
when he was a schoolboy,
when both he and Pakistan
were full of possibility.

He claims his memory
is failing, but the song rolls off
his tongue
with such ease I can't help
imagine him suddenly transported
back in time
when Indian films
could ignore history and dwell
on simpler things,
like love.

When my father's song
goes quiet, I pretend his silence
is due to forgetfulness.
I fail to realize
that his eyes have fallen
through the dark
bubbling surface of the tea
and found
for just a moment
the face of his father,
a man who long ago taught
my father this song,
sang it every morning
until the day he disappeared.

THE GIFT

Once, while dreaming about Lahore,
as I staggered over wet cobblestone
        toward the Wazir Khan Masjid sitting
in all its hidden grandeur buried within
        the labyrinth of the Walled City,
a man turbaned in red stepped from some
        invisible door into my path,
stopped me cold by grabbing my hand.
        Even in the gauzy rain of the dream, I felt
neither surprise nor panic, knowing all
        too well the wily tactics of street
merchants. I looked for clues to what he was
        selling, found only, gracing his pinky,
a ring I knew belonged to my father's
        father from having spent my childhood
studying my aunt's drawing of it hanging,
        framed in armour, in her dimly lit
apartment in Chicago. Before I could look
        up at the grandfather who left the living
world two decades before my birth,
        whose face I had only seen captured
in pencil, he released my fingers, spun away into
        the sparkling air, leaving me snatching
at mist. When I opened my other hand,
        it was there, exactly as I knew it –
but mine now, no longer possessed by the pain
        of mystery. I slipped it away as I entered
the mosque's courtyard where I prayed
        in my own sphere of longing, the wet
ground a touch of calm against my forehead.
        I stayed after the imam finished

leading the congregation, offered two extra
     awestruck rakahs in gratitude,
then sat at the edge of the smoldering sky
     reflected in the ablution pool to admire
with grief-weighted eyes this gift, tracing
     his first initial, the same as mine,
etched in the black stone nesting
     in silver. I swallowed the ring,
a careless act of hunger. And when I woke
     empty-handed, I could still feel it
burning in my blood, an ember,
     a comfort, a compass.

MY MOTHER'S DARKNESS

*…as perhaps at midnight, when all boundaries are lost, the country reverts to
its ancient shape, as the Romans saw it, lying cloudy, when they landed, and
the hills had no names and the rivers wound they knew not where – such was
her darkness…*

– Mrs Dalloway

On the roof of her childhood home on the outskirts of a
city once called Lyallpur sat a small storeroom where in
the colder months the family kept the charpoys on which
during summer nights the children slept, the stars sequined
to the sky the last wonders they saw before drifting into
sleep, the jute weave sagging beneath the weight of their
tired, dream-starved bodies. The wooden frames held the
etched initials of her oldest brothers all of whom had left
in a flourish of garlands and goodbyes for The New World
years before she understood the thrum of true longing, a
constant whir of an inner twilight humming through her
marrow, while along the surface of her forearms and face
there shone a melancholic radiance, the metallic blue skin
of a fish.

Sometimes, when everyone else napped in the cooler
confines of her parents' bedroom where the teak shutters
let in thin ribbons of flayed sunlight, my mother crept
upstairs and, gulping down her fear of spiders and jinn,
slipped into the darkness of the storeroom and stood
amongst the charpoys, propped up like massive books,
each cataloguing the mysteries of the Unseen world,
replete with cartographic riddles and the secret names
of oceans comprised of dead voices. There, a blank
page, she listened to a scattershot of sounds filling up the
empty lantern of her head – a machete hacking stalks of

sugarcane, a merchant hawking wire-sliced slabs of ice from his shop across the street, the clopping of a horse-drawn carriage ambling from one somewhere to another, even the soft cellular clicking of young bones growing toward something akin to transcendence.

Only a girl then, the youngest of four sisters, she loved the penetrating stillness of the afternoon, when Pakistan suffered at the brute hands of summer's fury and she found comfort in the way the entire universe grew soft like butter, when the edges of every wall and door, of every envelope sent from New York, Washington, London, Chicago, began to blur in the heat, when the solidity of every guardian tree or clump of earth lying upon the fresh graves in the cemetery wilted into dust, into the material from which everything sprouts upward toward heaven's sweet beckoning.

She squeezed shut her eyes, plugged her ears, and found a space far from the interrupting orbits of loud-mouthed scientists and holy men. And there she pretended to dissolve too, waiting for the atoms of her body to loosen their hold on one another, to rush apart in search of new galaxies to call home, for the glowing plumes of her soul to wisp into the air like the gauzy yarn of an unraveling pashmina, for that hum of longing to commune with the wind-borne breath of every being, be it a now-gone thing, or one not yet birthed – such was the might and measure of her darkness.

23

And her mind, at times feral from having lived as the youngest girl in a crowded home, in a country still mourning the loss of Jinnah decades after his passing, had discovered it could, within the sphere of her own inner burning, exist in every place on earth, in every moment of history at once. Within, she could mount undiscovered hills she would name after her favorite dolls – *Hawa, Majnoon, Lakshmi, Minerva, Clarissa* – and ride the meander of newborn rivers who shared their nascent journeys with no one but her. Inside this chamber, this storeroom on the roof of her family's home, a perpetual midnight endured, a time forever wedged in that liminal murk from which sprang the primordial voyages of clouds taking shape in the sky.

By the time her marriage had been arranged to the man who would become my father, my mother knew him already, had met him several times within the everywhereness of wonder, had come to know through his bleary eyes the grief-stricken coasts of the South China Sea, of Lake Michigan, of his own oceanic pain that traced its beginning to 1947; had come to know enough Cantonese and English to understand the agony embedded in his sleeping blabber, to recognize which ghost lurking behind the shimmer of his smile was his father's. Long before she saw him in the flesh, when all he was was a black-and-white photograph hidden beneath her pillow, she had plucked the mole at the corner of his mouth and planted it in the center of her heart, recast it into a private qibla, deciding that, like the universe itself, her own possible lives – her pasts, presents, futures – could all be found, invented, transformed, perhaps even understood as blessings, in the simplified calculus of darkness.

If – she decided – my eyes cannot grasp anything because there is no light, then what *can't* I see, what *can't* I claim?

FAISALABAD

At your feet, I wish for my death.
I pray for nothing else.
– from the poem, 'Nit Khair Manga' by Badar Ali Saheb Ansari.
Read while listening to a qawwali by Nusrat Fateh Ali Khan.

My mother's city and I
were both named
after an assassinated
Saudi king.

Before that, it was called
Lyallpur, after Sir James Broadwood Lyall,
former lieutenant governor
of the Punjab. He'd come east to India
to make a name for himself.

Nusrat learned to sing
in this city, is buried in this city.
When he died too soon,
two days after Independence Day 1997,
as the nation of Pakistan was still
celebrating its golden birthday,
many mourners smashed the time-
pieces in their homes,
as if to hold that day in place forever,
both the triumph of it
and the tragedy.

The trajectory of murder
began in the blood.
The assassin was a prince,

the king's nephew.
He knelt to kiss the king's feet,
then pulled out the gun.

Like neophytes newly planted on the earth,
the British were obsessed
with tangible things, like land and coin,
tea leaf and tongue, believed time
too could be colonized.
They replaced their blue-eyed God
with a devotion to the immortality
of their own tribe.
They built a new city, its orderly plan bereft
of the chaos so beautiful
to Punjabi souls, and placed at its epicenter
a clock tower, the perfect idol.

Was it really piety that addled
the king's sense of caution,
or was it a private pathway toward
holiness? The nephew
had confessed his designs
in time to be stopped,
but the king reminded people
that even he was mortal. That all things,
none more sacred than
life itself, rest in God's hands.

Nusrat's legacy is continued
by his nephew. His name is Rahat.
My mother's name is Rahat.
Heaven, Muslims believe,
lies beneath a mother's feet. I fall short
of them every moment of my life.

Radiating outward from its circular heart
are eight perfectly straight
streets, giant swords dividing the city
into eight mohallas,
each with its own name, its own magic
and music. From above,
from the vantage point
of dead souls floating heavenward,
the layout is a visual echo of the Union Jack.
As if the British understood
that to truly claim a place, it must be made
in one's own image.

Rahat means *respite,*
repose – and
to rest in peace
while one is still
a living thing.

What if I told you
the king's assassin
bore the same name
as the king?

Today, the city is proudly nicknamed
the Manchester
of Pakistan. I can't help
but imagine the dust
of Lyall's decayed flesh
resting in its grave,
smiling at the tightness
of the colonial noose, how it's now held
within the hands of the one
around whose neck

it hangs.
I share my name
with both an assassinated king
and his assassin.
My father's mother chose my name
against my mother's wishes.
My mother must have understood the double-edged
sting of the name, which means
judge, decision maker.
My mother decided, for her,
it would mean *home.*

In Urdu, the clock tower
is called Ghanta Ghar, meaning Hour House,
which sounds just like *our house.*
However, nothing of it is ours.

There are no better cures for homesickness
than Nusrat's qawwalis,
except when you're a mother
and you find comfort in the unfolding
hours of a child's existence.

As he lay dying
the king asked that his nephew's life
be spared. Again,
he said, Let God's will
execute itself.
No one of consequence listened,
believing the two bullets in his head,
the loss of blood,
rendered him foolhardy.
Hours later he was gone, his wish
unwished.

To rename a thing
is an attempt to undo whatever
unwantedness remains.
I wonder if, like this city, I too was
renamed – wonder what part
of the me that was
was unwanted.

Perhaps that's why they beheaded the nephew
on live television, then displayed
his crownless head for the world to see,
as if trying to show, through
the bewilderment on the dead man's disembodied face,
that all that's needed
to unfasten your grip on this world
is a sword, and someone willing to swing it.

You can see the faces
of the tower from any of the eight streets,
but the people of this city know not to trust
the time. Independence,
they say, began with the destruction
of clocks – or perhaps no one cares any longer
to fix what is broken – and so
it is assumed that whatever the faces say
must be wrong.

Sir Lyall is buried
in the English village of
Eastry, *of the east*.

Even now, there is a historian
in the city, once

a bookseller in Aminpur Bazar
and a devotee of Bhagat Singh,
who remains a sad-faced thing
stationed in his shuttered drawing room,
seeking in the living voice
of the dead King of Kings some excuse
for life. Qawwalis play
on a cassette deck, and on the wall
the Lifebuoy soap calendar,
untouched since that August day,
will one day become
someone else's
inheritance of grief.

BHAGAT SINGH

The man who goes on hunger strike has a soul. He is moved by that soul,
and he believes in the justice of his cause… However much you deplore them,
and however much you say they are misguided, it is the system, this damnable
system of governance, which is resented by the people.
– Muhammad Ali Jinnah (1929)

With batons they beat his comrade
Lala Lajpat Rai, whose heart would surrender

to the blows. In the foam spilling
from the dying man's mouth Bhagat heard

the voices of Douglass and Du Bois,
and he wept at the sheer nobility of the oppressed,

be they Indian or American, and thereafter
he resolved to die a free man.

That the Angrez so wholeheartedly believed
their blue eyes were celestial favors

rubbed him all wrong. They were first-class
thieves, the whole lot, and it mattered

not what their laws said about revolution,
nor which of them caught a bullet.

If it would cost him his life to reclaim
his life, then why hesitate? I can kill you too,

he shouted, and I will. And he did,
despite the Mahatma's insistence on nonviolence.

His version of dignity had room enough
for bombs. For bludgeoning hunger and thirst.

For 116 days he refused all sustenance,
and in the hallucinations that ensued,

his soul traveled to Mount Meru
where it spoke directly to Guru Nanak,

who asserted there is nothing holier
in God's eyes than Truth. But Bhagat Singh

blinked away the vision, insisting
the only real truth was a man's own self.

At twenty-three, he and two others were hanged
in Lahore, their bodies secretly cremated at night,

their ashes tossed into the Sutlej River
just as dawn was breaking.

PRAYER

you cleanse the uncovered
regions of your body
then stand at the foot
of prayer mats facing

the qibla unfasten
your cluttered mind
from the tangible hold of secular
trances bow down

before the cascading
glow of God's mercy submit
to a centripetal course toward the gates
of a more perfect emptiness

here now
you can plunge into the most secluded
chamber of the soul commune
with your share of the universe's

initial burst of light eternal light
housed within the lamp of mystery
waiting to be
beheld five times a day

AYODHYA

After the Babri Masjid Massacre
Ayodhya, India, December 1992

Knowing you so well, Hisham,
you must have been sitting at an old wooden desk,
hiding behind a wall of books, contemplating
the unifying potential of Rumi's poems
when the rioting suddenly broke, when the mobs flooded
the streets, heading straight toward the Babri —
that cursed house of God long evacuated
and left to crumble under the weight of the centuries.
That afternoon, children were exiled
into the bowels of misunderstood history, suffering
from the inheritance of their parents' grievances.
Hypnotized by stories that spoke of imaginary pasts,
of holy birthplaces and forgotten birthrights,
they ripped through Ayodhya, roaring like a stampede
of elephants, thirsty for the taste of a brother's blood.
Convinced only a divine decree could inspire
so many to suddenly become so God-conscious,
even the most simple-minded onlookers
must have felt compelled to join in, to help dismantle
one version of history, brick by brick, bone by bone.
When darkness finally fell on our city, falling like a black veil,
as if trying to keep the stars from bearing witness
to this unholy event, from this suicidal December day,
the demolished edifice was mere backdrop.
The 3,000 corpses were what reminded us
that Ayodhya would belong to no one anymore.

Yet this city was still ours —
we grew up here, misfits who spent our days in the streets,

our nights sneaking off to the movie houses
to see our boy-dreams projected onto movie screens
as wide as the night. This is our Ayodhya.
Here we attended the same school our fathers did,
the one behind the dilapidated church, peopled by the poor
Hindu-converts who were fooled into believing
that Jesus was born blue – that the name
Krishna was rooted in the words *Christ* and *Christian*.
That was our Ayodhya. Do you remember
how we longed for school to end each afternoon,
suffering through the schoolmasters' thrashes,
generously intended to subdue our perpetual impatience?
We couldn't wait to go hide behind Black Joseph's
sweetmeat stand, positioned perfectly to steal quick glances
at the girls blossoming in our neighborhood.
Remember how boyishly we battled over Nargis,
the girl we renamed after the film goddess?
She taught us the meaning of lust
by occasionally winking at us with her dark eyes,
making us hard between the legs.
Do you remember how Black Joseph,
whenever he saw us eyeing Nargis, our crotches
pressed up against his stand, would sing songs stolen
from films – songs our fathers sang to us long
before we understood the meaning of heartache and loss
and memory? And how, lost in musical reveries,
Black Joseph, hands on hips, would whirl
like a drunk dervish, mocking us with his fluttering eyelashes?
How whenever he laughed he would be overcome
by a bout of coughing so violent he had to hold onto his
dhoti to keep it from falling to his feet?

Hisham, do you remember the sweet scent
of the mango trees on my uncle's farm in Amritsar,

their thick leaves dangling elegantly like earrings
from the ears of Queen Noor Jahan? Do you know
why we never went back there? Outside,
under their generous shade – in a darkness so viscous
it held us like a black net – we remained unaware
of the turbulence raging in my uncle's kitchen.
We never heard him cursing wildly, throwing guilt and history
in my father's face, who, I learned many years later,
had dared to bring a Muslim into a Brahmin home,
who threatened our family name with an unwashable stain.
My father – who always called your father *Bhaiya*
and taught me to call you by the same brotherly name –
never spoke back, allowed his brother-in-law
to beg Lord Krishna's blue face to curse my family
with sickness and a shameful legacy of barren daughters-in-law.
Protected from the sweltering summer sky
by the mango trees, we enjoyed our youthful ignorance,
counted the ants crawling up our legs,
and eventually admitted drowsiness, the heat heavy
on our eyelids, pushing them down, slowly until shut.
I leaned back in my charpoy, rested my head in my hands.
Between the dull thudding of ripe mangoes
falling to the ground, I enjoyed the calming silence
of your sleep, and dreamed away the restlessness
I sometimes saw dancing in my mother's eyes.

My friend, it is a shame our mothers didn't talk more.
They both suffered from the same epidemic of silence,
a clinging to a nameless injury, one no words would heal,
one no amount of forgetting could ever undo.
I remember one Friday afternoon, when you disappeared
with your father into a masjid near the vacant Babri,
my mother asked that I come home to help her
chop greens for dinner. We were expecting company,

old family friends, people too important to disappoint,
and I was expected to sit silently, godlike
in the corner of the room, watchful, smiling, dead
to the living. After a morning of street cricket
and wrestling in the dusty school gardens, my face was dark
with dirt, and mud stained my clothes – I looked
like a beggar, absolutely shameful. My mother
joked that I was too filthy to be her son.
As she washed my face, her hands kneading at my skin,
she let a long, deep sigh betray her smile.
When I asked her why her eyes looked
so all-of-a-sudden dim, her face became the sun,
no longer sad. She said she just preferred that I spend
more time indoors, out of reach of the sun's summer fury,
which – if I wasn't careful – would make me
dark-skinned forever, like an untouchable.

When your wife Jamila begged you to forget
Ayodhya, to find a teaching post in Lahore,
where Urdu's best writers spent their evenings
at the Pak Tea House – at least for your unborn children
if not for her – you pressed your body hard against hers
to still the heaving of her chest. You knew she had never felt
at home in India, had begged you since your wedding night
to do as her parents had done and migrate away
to Pakistan. But you refused to flee. You would not
tolerate her mistrust of Hindus, would not fall victim to a history
flooded with misinterpretations. In your eyes,
the mistake of Partition had disfigured the Subcontinent,
had left this land wounded, aching, fractured, forever searching
for wholeness. Now she curses your relentless optimism
and wishes to forget your ghost, which she sees forever
in your son's eyes. Bilal must be in school now, a small prince
of a boy who will soon inherit the poison of a mother's suffering.

Hisham, when you were killed outside the Babri,
in the aftermath of the storm that bathed our city with blood,
each drop in the name of one god or another,
I fell against the wall, torn apart, mumbles of some broken language
spilling from my fumbling lips. With an aggression
that gave me nightmares for weeks, I seized the statues
my parents had given me, so placid and silent
on bookshelves and tabletops, no longer worthy
of my trust, and flung them to the floor.
Decapitated heads, amputated arms, severed legs flew
in all directions, in splashes of marble, stone, and porcelain.
My body quivered with the disease, and I considered
prying out my eyes with my fingers, pushed
hard enough to see explosive red flares colliding
against the backs of my eyelids. Then I disappeared
to find you – *but all I saw were faces, glowing,*
alive with fury. Faces broken and blinking, without
sequence, like film clips sewn together haphazardly – faces
lost in time, in slow-motion, overlapping, becoming
the same face. Faces white with fear, flowering with a flourish
of curses, some lips spewing spit, mixed with blood, dust.
Others stitched shut, with voices clogged in windpipes,
the muffled sounds of gagging and suffocation reverberating
through the alleys. I saw faces with eyes gouged out,
limp optic nerves hanging flaccidly from empty eye sockets.
Faces singed, seared onto corpses, strewn through the streets,
left for the dogs to manage. Faces full of tears, shame,
happiness, disbelief. For a moment, I thought I saw your face,
one of the many, a transient flame, flickering, fading fast,
engulfed by even larger flames, consumed by chaos,
disappearing completely, drowned in a sea of other faces –
forever lost, forever lost.

My dead brother, Ayodhya suffers without you,
continues to tear open its own wounds, and I no longer know
what to believe in. The difficulty of Ghalib's poems
brought us together at school, while Amitabh Bhachan
united us in the evenings in film. He was the hero of our lives,
defying the test of time in movie after movie,
handsome as ever, the only true actor-singer
Bollywood has ever known. His *Namak Halal* was our favorite,
with the crazy action sequences in which he would defeat
the weakling villains, each with a single punch.
We wanted to be him – or just like him
since we'd have preferred to kiss the heroine at the end.
But such were the storyline formulas of Indian cinema –
nothing could ever be changed, and we knew
to let our dreams continue the story, to complete the vacancies
that perforated our lives. We were just two boys
too close to notice the differences that would fall between us
like worlds, two friends growing up, learning to absorb
the tremors of inheritance, the rhythmic pounding of
clashing histories, remaining unshaken, never questioning
the motherly silences that congealed in our memories,
that became stones that sunk into the sands of
our forgetting. Perhaps nothing has brought people so much
sadness through the centuries than these religions,
these solemn ways of life, death, and indifference.
And our abbreviated brotherhood was blessed
to have such perceptive fathers who shielded us
from the foolishness that accompanied
blind faith, who taught us that new partitions
would not help us unravel our convoluted pasts.

Yes, Bhaiya, every year as a stranger I come to Ayodhya
under quiet circumstances – just the wind and me –
to keep myself from forgetting you. Yet I pray

for forgetfulness here, for some way to erase the events of
that bloody December, which replay themselves in my nightmares,
frame by frame. I have learned from the violence
that still stains our soil, that no one ever forgets
the things that must be forgotten. Forgetting, a kind of forgiveness,
eludes our people, keeps them helplessly bound to pain,
so easily ignited into bursts of hateful action.
Visiting you helps purge my despair, instills in me
a new kind of hope, one that propels me back
into my incomplete life in a faraway city. I have left Ayodhya
many times, and in leaving I continue to live.
This is a city still devoid of faith, a city wounded
and bleeding, a city once ours to trust, once ours to pass on.
I press my ears against your tombstone, flat on the ground –
closer to you. I feel its cold hardness and listen
for our fathers' songs to rise like phantoms from the earth.
From this fallen position I remember your voice,
remember how you impersonated Mohammad Rafi
with effortless precision, while I stretched to be Lata,
as we sang together the old songs, once again
unstaging the tragedy of time. On the train home,
whenever my body begins convulsing in tremors of sadness,
these songs console my lostfulness and save me
from weeping loudly in the company of strangers.

THE FACES OF THE HOLY

for heaven loves the struggle and the brave
faces of fiction, and no one
no one will look upon the holy, for
the face of the holy is ashes and smoke.
– from 'The Faces, Up There' by Helen Degen Cohen

How can the human heart, without ripping apart at the seams,
Ever house the immeasurable heartache of one's own history? Every
Life carries a library of loss, dark corridors lined with the never-
Ending almanacs of tragedy, yes. But where are the ones whose holy
Nature compels them to sing of the ashes and smoke, to render

Destruction into something worth remembering, perhaps
Even beautiful when held against the fire? They walk amongst us,
Guided by the voices of the dead, collecting windswept scraps of grief,
Exhuming from the silences the skeletal remains of ancestors whose
Names must be invented, reanimated by language. And as poets

Communing every night with the angels of history, heaven
Opens its gates for them, gives each a turn to glance inside, to touch
Hands with the lost, to hear the unutterable prayers of the living
Echoing through their own yearning, even in death. This is what we
Now know is holiness, to heal the unhealable anguish of others.

DENATURALIZATION: AN ELEGY FOR MR VAISHNO DAS BAGAI, AN AMERICAN

Now what am I? What have I made of myself and my children? We cannot exercise our rights. Humility and insults, who is responsible for all this? Me and the American government [...] Obstacles this way, blockades that way, and bridges burnt behind.

– from Vaishno Das Bagai's suicide letter, *San Francisco Examiner,* March 17, 1928

1. INNER LIGHT

As a boy, visiting blood
          in the warmer regions

of Hindustan, bursting
          with a sorrow he did not

yet understand, he stuffed
          his mouth with the fire

of fireflies, haunting
          his bemused cousins

with a flickering
          smile, all teeth and flint

spark. Before they drowned
          in the spit of unspoken

wishes, he gulped them
          down, believing, thanks

to the delicious God-bending
          bak-bak of his best friend,

Mohammad, a princely Pathan,
          eyes bewitched by

a marrow-deep lust
          for independence,

that the swallowed magic
          of their light would guide

his ache-shackled
          heart toward a purer

promise of home waiting
          beyond the untouchable

hunger of this stolen land's
          stolen futures,

in a place perfected by freedom
          and christened America.

2. SAN FRANCISCO

For thirteen years he woke
haunted by the dreamt-of smells
of Peshawar – his father's

neem-fragrant breath, his mother's
hair, its coconut oil–pungent
blooming comfort, the punch

of gardenia ghosting through
night's fragile stillness. Sometimes
even the kneeling crave of sun-

baked water-buffalo dung burning
beneath an immense copper
daig of moong daal, enough

to feed every hunger-striking
prisoner back home or to last until
the first blare of Judgment Day's

trumpet call, until the bladed
shards of a shattered American sky
smashed against his brown face.

His wife, Kala, their three sons,
had allowed Bagai to forsake Brahma,
to turn his faith toward the blue-

eyed gods of Transformation
who had greeted them at the gates
of Angel Island with flameless

lanterns, festering wounds to mark
the sites of amputated wings.
Kala had given into the delusion too,

had, out of mercy, learned to bite
her cautioning tongue, to silence doubt,
to sweet-talk away the undeniable –

that one day her husband's blood
would mount the most vicious
testimony against him.

3. THE CHINESE

Some of the ones
      loitering in the streets
of California look to me
      like dirty catfish.

Perhaps that is why
      the goras are so afraid
they carry a taint pursed
      behind slashed eyes.

The first time I met one –
      a nomadic herbalist
en route to Kabul
      where a girl he'd met

two years before
      waited for his return –
he asked me, mouthing
      each labored

word of English
      as if spitting out
a clod of cold earth,
      if I had a spare shilling

to purchase for him
      a few sips of salvation.
As he drank water
      from a bhisti's spout,

water I paid for,
      not out of kindness
but a towering gut-swell
      of pity, he promised

he'd return to Peshawar,
      he and his bride-
to-be, and pay back
      his debt in gift.

These days, whenever
      one of them spits
at Kala's feet for wearing
      her sari in public,

or daring to flaunt
      the nose diamond
with the audacity
      of the newly emancipated,

I touch the heavenly
      silk flower hidden
in my pocket
      to remember the strange

beauty of that man's spirit,
      and the quiet
might I beheld in the smiling
      incandescence

of his wife's
      face, round as the moon.
Then I drown
      in long swigs of silence

to vanquish the rage
        and despair, embering
within the throats
        of my fellow American-

souled 'Asiatics'
        as we battle the ugly self-
annihilation prowling
        in every mirror,

hungry, ready
        to pounce, to devour
our hearts from
        the inside out.

4. UNITED STATES V. BHAGAT SINGH THIND (1923)

Mr Justice Sutherland, white
America requests you, an immigrant

from Great Britain, but now
a naturalized citizen of these great

United States of America,
to please, if you may, answer –

with an absence of smirk
(the unflinching angels of history

are watching us, Your Honor) –
the following two questions:

1. Is a high-caste Hindu of full Indian blood,
born at Amrit Sar, Punjab, India,
a white person?

2. Does the Immigration Act of February 5, 1917,
disqualify from naturalization as citizens
those Hindus, now barred by that act,
who had lawfully entered the United States
prior to the passage of said act?

It may be true that the blond
Scandinavian and the brown Hindu
have a common ancestor in the dim
reaches of antiquity, but the average
man knows perfectly well that
there are unmistakable and profound

differences between them today…
It is a matter of familiar observation
and knowledge that the physical
group characteristics of the Hindus
render them readily distinguishable
from the various groups of persons

in this country commonly recognized
as white. The children of English,
French, German, Italian, Scandinavian
and other European parentage quickly
merge into the mass of our population
and lose the distinctive hallmarks

of their European origins. On the other
hand, it cannot be doubted that the children
born in this country of Hindu parents

would retain indefinitely the clear
        evidence of their ancestry. It is very far
from our thought to suggest the slightest

        question of racial superiority or inferiority.
What we suggest is merely racial
        difference, and it is of such character
and extent that the great body
        of our people instinctively recognize it
and reject the thought of assimilation.

5. DENATURALIZATION

Sometimes they revert to trickery, apple their venom
        with a smile, hide serpent tongues behind

cages of teeth. Bagai understood banishment, the fall
        from air perfumed by imagined dignity,

his lungs blackened by the scorch of bridges burnt.
        The British ruined him long before America

got its chance to, but blindness costs nothing,
        not when tomorrow holds out two hands, one

to cloak each eye. So one morning, in the familiar choke-
        hold of his office on Fillmore, as Bagai stood

half-dead already in a diminishing island of sunlight,
        once again fighting off the demons of a home-facing

nostalgia, a pudgy ruddy-cheeked associate – Adams,
        born of Adams and before him another such

Adams, all the way back to Adam himself – blew open
      Bagai's heart with a newspaper, carefully folded

to display a weaponized headline. Adams' finger
      stabbed the words, spoke, in the desert lilt of eastern

California, of the lunacy of Bagai's people. 'Such
      blasphemy', said Adams, launching into a lurching

diatribe about this turbaned 'hindoo' who, with the tenacity
      only a crazy man could muster, claimed *whiteness*

against the shouting protests of his dark skin, against
      the thickening tangle of the nation's self-cleansing

combustibility. Adams, appalled and apple-eyed,
      lost himself in wobbling laughter. Bagai seized

the newspaper, retreated to the window, and felt his skin
      begin to dissolve, while down below, a knot

of Chinese laborers shared a pipe, inhaling deeply the white
      smoke, their longing unbuttoned from home-

starved souls by opium's hushed mercy. Bagai continued
      to read: this 'hindoo', Thind, was in fact a Sikh,

a veteran of the U.S. Army, a lover of Whitman, Emerson,
      and Thoreau. A 'Caucasian' on account of his

Punjabi birth, made and unmade as a citizen, had been
      shoved by the courts into a sacrificial spotlight,

becoming the national face of denaturalization, a goat
        placed throat-up before the butcher. Adams

son of Adams, snatched back the paper, narrowed
        the dead blue of his eyes into knives, spoke now

of the limits of desire, a touch too gleefully for Bagai's
        withering sense of pride. Or perhaps Adams' pluckiness

was another trick Bagai had fallen for, his heart-rending
        want so deep it had become accustomed

to recasting every tongue-slap of poison into song.
        And when his Berkeley neighbors shuttered the doors

of his newly mortgaged Eden-to-be, he understood Adams'
        warning, understood exactly what even the Supreme

Court of this nation found so untouchable about his kind.
        The blindfold had unraveled. He did not pick up

a chisel to loosen the planks, nor attempt to diffuse hate
        by showcasing the bona fide radiance of his sweet

salesman smile. Instead, he swallowed another defeat,
        felt his soul turn slowly toward his now-dead childhood

friend Mohammad, and began, within the gathering
        darkness of despair, to script a reunion. Bagai, penned

in by shadows, glared at the newspaper Adams had left behind,
        and saw the truth: that despite whatever bargain

he tried to strike with the devil, he had never been –
        and would never be – an American. His was a different

displacement, hovering along the blade-edge of grief,
        banished on account of his unchangeable blood.

6. WHAT BURNS

over the next few years   as his eyes adjusted
to the misty smoke   screen light
of Paradise   to promises that animal a man's
self-worth   to the slithering

deception of America's beckon   Bagai saw beyond
the tears   beyond the treachery of longing
bridging one lost home   to another
recognized   the knife-glint

of every wingless tomorrow   by the time he'd finished
his morning   cup of tea
its gingered throb a purifying fire   in his heart's
haunted chambers   untethered from the Raj

he pledged a new   allegiance to his flag
to the Republic   for which it stands
one nation   indivisible
with liberty and justice   for –

he felt more soul-spent   than lost
yet as he knotted   his tie for what he understood
would be the last time   he wondered
if perhaps   it might be better

to imposter
to that previous
where one could find comfort
could still dream

where he'd happily face
eyes of the Angrez
of his dead
for a chance to whip him

for wanting to be
of light
locked up
ultimately

executioner
brave until the bitter end
even when it descends into sin
that to take your own life

his way back
captivity
in the promise of inferiority
of independence as attainable

the firing-squad
of the blood he'd forsaken
parents' spirits aching
once again

filled with a different shade
a bird now
in a gilded cage
he decided to be his own

a true American
believing democracy
offers a path to dignity
is the only way to die free

7. 'MORAL GESTURE'

Feeling trapped and betrayed, Vaishno went to San Jose alone on a business pretext, rented a room there, and took his own life by gas poisoning.

– Rani Bagai, granddaughter

And so

as his soul

migrates

from

the earthy depths

of his broken

body

into

the white noise

of death,

behind him

an echo of light

a scarlet tanager

perched

at a window

beyond

his sphere

of vision

wings so blooded

with fire

their departure

a red flash

on the wall

he evaporates

into the life-

affirming lure

of poison-

rich air

8. RESTORATION

Then the voice –
        Mohammad's,
               long ago silenced

by bullet – lifting
        from the smoke: Brother,
               welcome home

to despair, to the power
        held within it.
               Let's surrender

to the perfected
        beauty of our inner
               light, converge

as cloud enshrouding
        the shoulders
               of the holy mountains

of our youth,
        become the sweetness
               of rain, the enduring

innocence
        of silk flowers.
               Let the atoms

of our exiled
        existences mingle
               again in the ether

beneath the burning
　　　　gaze of the Almighty,
　　　　　　　into whose lovely

mouth we may still
　　　　return, our souls
　　　　　　　like the fireflies

that filled our
　　　　bellies as boys,
　　　　　　　their swallowed light

convincing us,
　　　　as we took our last
　　　　　　　breath as brave men,

that rivers of pain
　　　　had purified
　　　　　　　our longing,

given our bloodlines
　　　　an undeniable
　　　　　　　claim upon whatever

nation or delusion
　　　　to which they wedded
　　　　　　　their perishable orbits,

for which they sacrificed
　　　　their innate holiness, all
　　　　　　　for a taste of might.

IN DEFENSE OF MONSTERS

What the image does not show is that I had talked to other witnesses to try and find out what was happening, to see if I could be of any help, even though enough people were at the scene tending to the victims. I then decided to call my family to say that I was fine and was making my way home from work, assisting a lady along the way by helping her get to Waterloo station. My thoughts go out to all the victims and their families. I would like to thank Jamie Lorriman, the photographer who took the picture, for speaking to the media in my defence.
– The Muslim woman on Westminster Bridge, London, March 22, 2017

Let them monster the world's Muslims, monster our pain
by saying we pay no mind, monster our living hurt

with the phantom aches they've fabricated in factories that once,
in some dream, produced goods good enough to rival

God's own work. Let them monster their invented heartache,
grafting it onto the living hurts that their own kind rubbled

into their lives, leaving them so broken their eyes had nowhere safe
to turn except onto our faces whose incandescent beauty

filled them with such massive libraries of shame they needed
again the native strength of our shoulders to carry

their brittle bodies into others' regions of panic. They'll conquer
and concoct new names for these lands, too, thieving

with one invented victory after another any claim we hold
to goodness. Let them monster us and those who survived before us

and continue to survive the monstering, be it as living things
on a bridge beneath the gaze of Big Ben, in mosques

in Canada and America and Pakistan and Yemen and Iran
and Palestine and Myanmar and Germany and China

where our blood on the sidewalk, the wall, the window, the front
page of the newspaper, the back page of policy, is our burden

to wash. And so on and so forth on battered battlegrounds
where our own bodies have been blown to bits by the monsters

who claim our names and turn to the monstering ones
and say, Raise us up as your saviors, and make us your healing

flames. Let them be saved by such imposters whose bloody crimes
nourish their monstering minds, guide their monstering hands

as they sculpt, from the thin air of worry, towers of fear,
rejection, exclusion, law, and more and more cries for war,

for bombs, for the absolute annihilation of us. Let them monster
their own monstering, monster their own laundered history,

trading one monster for another, surrendering once again,
but this time with flailing arms and drowning soul,

to the monsters in their blood. Let them monster any explosive word
we might utter in protest, or in compassion, or in self-

healing, until it's a silenced angel, for – don't you understand yet? –
when they've already monstered us beyond recognition,

we might as well just swallow the pain of being monstered,
help some old lady cross the street, away from the destruction,

do that instead of fighting back, then plunge into the obliterating
rush of the subway. What better way to let them monster

their own destinies and the promised greatness of their oversold
tomorrows. Let them be free to monster every great nation

that promises better, monster the goodness of these lands,
monster the earth living beyond the flay of their shortsightedness,

monster God Himself until what's left is nothing but
the monstering darkness of their own cries, cutting through

the cruel echoes of their dying breaths, their final pleas for tolerance,
or something like that, reverberating through the silence.

ADVICE TO RELIGIOUS FANATICS

chill
the
fuck
out

please

for
God's
sake

WHENEVER HE TEACHES *HAMLET*

He forgets the tune to his baby boy's favorite
lullaby. He forgets to fasten his seatbelt before
        driving away. He forgets to dog-ear the spot
where he gave up on another self-help book.
        He forgets that stillness does not mean you stop

breathing. He forgets to put the leftovers in
        the fridge, to soak the pots and pans. He forgets
to feed his family of pet goldfish, forgets to say
        their names before leaving for work. He forgets
that Hamlet once had a father, too. He forgets

        which way is Mecca. He forgets his best friend's
name, forgets to ask about his dying cat, about
        his dying tomatoes. He forgets he doesn't believe
in ghosts. He forgets to shampoo his hair, forgets
        he no longer has any hair. He forgets to pick up

the dry-cleaning, forgets to finish buttoning
        his shirt. He forgets to eat breakfast, forgets to
pack a lunch. He forgets to call his mother
        on her birthday. He forgets the anniversary of
his father's death. He forgets his phone at work,

        forgets to check his mailbox before leaving school.
He forgets to like a former professor's post about
        his newly published book of poems. He forgets
the man is slowly going blind. He forgets to pray
        the morning prayer until after the sun has risen.

He forgets to tell his students Hamlet is really not
          crazy, that it's all about the paralyzing pain of
a broken heart, of a grief that endures. He forgets
          to mail the check to the electric company, forgets
to set up automatic bill pay, forgets to ask if

          they might waive the late fee again. He forgets
nobody is supposed to remember everything.
          He forgets to take his vitamins. He forgets the Urdu
word for loneliness, forgets the Punjabi word for
          loneliness, forgets the English word for loneliness.

He forgets to post the homework assignment for
          his first period class, forgets to check work email
once he gets home, forgets Hamlet really isn't crazy,
          forgets not to blame the guy for being so heartbroken.
He forgets to brush his teeth before going to bed.

          He forgets to take out the bathroom trash, forgets
what it means to let go, to move on, to let memory
          bring comfort, not agony. He forgets it hurts
others when he forgets, forgets it hurts him
          when he hurts others with forgetting. He forgets

the password to his online banking account, forgets
          the cat has been dead for a long time, that those
tomatoes survived, and were quite sweet. He forgets
          his father in his final weeks asked him to clean his
childhood bedroom, to remove all his old books,

          forgets he's still not finished the job. He forgets to
tie his shoes, to zip his fly. He forgets how old he is.
          He forgets those are birds trilling in the tree outside
his window, not noisy angels on vacation. He forgets
          to wash the paper cut on his finger before putting

on a Band-Aid. He forgets to cry at the funeral,
	forgets to bring flowers, forgets to tell his mother
he is sorry. He forgets to tell his wife he is sorry.
	He forgets to tell his son, his students – the rest of
the world – he is sorry. He forgets the significance

	of Ramadan, forgets to wait for the sun to set
before breaking his fast with two dates and a glass
	of water, forgets to spit out the pits. He forgets to
show up for jury duty, forgets to reschedule, forgets
	if it's even possible to reschedule. He forgets he does

actually believe in ghosts, in giving them a chance
	to explain themselves. He forgets to buy diapers,
wipes, the right brand of fancy organic unsweetened
	almond milk from that new fresh market next to
the abandoned currency exchange. He forgets

	to get gas. Again, he forgets about poor Hamlet,
forgets a broken heart can undo even the most normal
	person's grip on things. He forgets that inside his heart,
where he thinks there is nothing, there sits a room
	where he can lock himself on days when he doesn't

know where else to go. He forgets he still remembers
	the words to the lullaby, that his son is old enough
now to help him remember the tune, to hold him
	together until the final scene when most everyone
dies and the living can finally go back home.

BEING IN TOUCH

Good morning –
I have just returned from NC. I spent a week with my friend
after Wildacres. I am now meeting my brothers in Wisconsin to
spread my mother's ashes. I'll be in touch when I return.
Blessings,
– Dora Robinson

Afterwards, I imagine the dust
of her life lingering on your fingertips,
wafting up into the sun-filled room
as you type off a quick note,
each mote a touch of her being,
a moment she spent alone
in her rocking chair, remembering.
Her favorite stories were yours.
Binge-drinking while cloistered
at that Chicago convent, blaming
the teargas and not the pain
when you cried during the riots
of '68. She told the world about
how you'd outwitted Daley all the way
to Texas only to find yourself
face-to-face with the Devil himself.
Even as a girl, you asked her impossible
questions about God and good
and giddiness, about the differences
between right and righteousness.
Her quiet smiles were her most honest
answers. You've left some of her
unfinished prayers on the laptop keys,
her being in touch. When the next
person sits there to write – perhaps

it will be one of your brothers,
or an old friend still alive in Wisconsin –
he will feel her papery skin there,
think of the way her cheeks glowed
in winter. If when your plane touches
down in Austin, the place feels
unfamiliar, and you finger away a tear
rising up from the past like a ghost,
think of how she will remain
on your face, a glitter more holy
than mere resemblance, a holiness
made tactile with remembrance.

THE SALVATION OF *AURELLA AURITA*

I check them every day to make sure
they're happy and in good shape.
– Dorothy B. Spangenberg, Ph.D.

Jellyfish born in space aren't happy
On earth. I don't believe in any hocus-pocus
New-age mumbo-jumbo, but I hurt for this

Species of boneless electric wonder
Named after the moon. Self-possessed by
A terrifying terrestrial bulk – *weight* –

They feel fat, slow, depressed, dying not
In the luminous white noise of galactic emptiness
But in casserole dishes, under-understood,

In some under-funded underground
NASA lab, poked by pencils, punctured despair
Seeping from their glassy globes. Perhaps

They pine for the way the weightlessness
Of space made them feel more like light bulbs
Than corpses. I'd trade my life for that

Delusion of worth. The future is cannibalistic
For glowing things dimmed. And space-born
Jellyfish-lungs ache when the bluster

Of breath pollutes the soul. Then what's left
To be saved? I say, rocket them homeward,
Through the incinerating mist of earth's atmosphere.

May their longing to be ethereal again
Cremate the damage of gravity. May the space dust
Of their pain dissipate into the gasping void.

LOST DOG: VERY AFRAID, DO NOT CHASE

The homemade paper sign hangs soggy
from a blossoming tree at the train station
and shows not a photograph of the poor
creature but a black water-blotched smear
of life, making me wonder about the dog's
actual whereabouts, if over-excited children
discovering it behind a bush, triggered
such a scare with their shrieks of joy that
instead of acquiescing to their rescuing arms
or sprinting off to another place to hide,
it simply puddled like ink at their feet
and seeped into the ground, given
a final chase by spring rain.

REMEMBERING STELLA AND LILY, WHO DIED ON THE SAME DAY

Solemnly you recognize, when measured by human time
That the lives of dogs are much too short, so you take
Each little second and make it seven, and do so out of
Love, a love so vast it needs more than a lifetime to claw
Loose the last layers of longing in a person's remembering.
And so you love them deeply and purely, at times with

An awe that transcends the reach of your own imagination.
Nobody else can understand the joys of this joy, of these
Dogs who, when death came, entered its embrace together,

Leaving in their wake, like the rocketing light of the stars,
Iridescence that undoes darkness and melancholy, whose
Lingering presence, charged by the lives they lived, makes
You feel they're still there, curled up at your feet, asleep.

ON THE MORNING OF NOVEMBER 9, 2016, I HAD AN ENTIRE PUMPKIN PIE FOR BREAKFAST

Yes, I started my day by eating
a whole pumpkin pie, cold, straight
from the tin while standing before
the open fridge, telling myself,
as the chilled air stilled my blood
and kept at bay more tears and sighs
laced with venom and hurt, that
nothing's wrong with being a woman
who eats with her fingers and makes
a mess at her feet, not when
no ceiling broke the night before,
when our nation elected *him* –
when to survive this day and the next
four years' worth will require many
more small, nourishing acts of self-
indulgence and sweet defiance.

AFTERWARDS

On the worst days, as I'm about to consume in secret
an entire assorted dozen while seated in my darkened kitchen,
armed with knife and fork, white handkerchief
noosed around my throat, an attempt, I guess, to give
the gluttony a touch of class, I think of each long john as a life
raft, the ringed others as lifesavers tossed into a sea
in which, after breaking half a dozen promises
and eyeing a half-dozen more, I've begun to drown,
not in the oily translucence lingering along the surface
of the box, but in knowing, once again, the delight
I found in the first surrender will be, with each subsequent bite,
a diminishing love, leaving me filled but unfulfilled.
I promise next time I'll buy only one, but know in my heart
that everything about donuts is a lie, that the best part
is their missing center, their resemblance to the me
I've become. When there's nothing left to sink
my shame into, I close my eyes, listen to my teeth sing,
lick the tip of my finger, and, in gentle jabs, search
the crumby tabletop for stray sprinkles, each hoping to be
found, eaten by a lonely someone who shares the pain of existing
on the glazed layer of someone else's idea of perfection.

THE FORGOTTEN BANANA

Perhaps I should feel sad
knowing I've become
a forgotten fruit, left behind
in the gathering darkness
of the school copy room.
There is solace to be found
in the hum of the humidifier,
the pulse-like clicks
of these massive machines
savoring this rare spell of rest.
It is a Friday, and beyond
the walls of my epic loneliness,
I wonder if anyone is still
looking for me, nursing
a sweet gut-panged
hankering for potassium
after a long day of teaching
and yearning. If someone
does claim me, may she be
a kind soul, peel away my skin
lovingly, enjoy the life
I've lived – a life destined
not to be a forgotten thing,
but something delicious,
something good.

LOST EARRING

With its
pearly gray
head
and that
shimmering
hickey of
light,
it looks
like a tadpole
lost, tiny
tail wriggling
in search
of its perch:
a lobe,
somewhere,
hanging
unadorned,
forlorn,
not just
an ear to it,
but a home.

WHAT AWAITS IS MADE MORE LUMINOUS
BY THE BLOOMING LIGHT OF YOUTH

Before the first silver thread of dawn appears, before their sleeping

Eyes horizon against the song-broken stillness of a new day,

Something beautiful and secret has begun to bloom within

The spongy hollows of their bones. If they lie unmoving a minute,

Without breath, without hunger, they might feel the grinning

Intensity of an untomorrowed day, the whir of every unlived hour,

Sugared more by wonder and awe than worry, cocooning them

Head to toe in sweetness, in the tender dangling curiosity of human

Existence. They must phoenix the shadows of yesterday's skin,

Stretch forth their emptiness, believe even the mothering sun,

Forever an untouchable thing, is touchable now. That is, if they

Remember eternity exists only in mirrors, that the delight of rapture

Originates in the liminal hum between stillness and the dizzying

Motion of growing up. It's the wild brilliance of youth that's so

Utterly blinding, that windows the soul, that becomes its own

Story life will write with a certainty their hands can't yet grasp.

ELLA FITZGERALD, ENTERING CHICAGO BY TRAIN, REMEMBERS HER MOTHER'S VOICE

Mother kept church
Songs tucked inside her
Brassière, warmed
By the bursting fullness
Of her bosom, and
Like candied wishes
She popped them,
One after another, in her
Mouth, and despite
The shyness we shared
Like blood and that
Forgotten history
Of our ancestors, she
Sang open the too-small
August mornings
Of Yonkers while doing
The laundry of olive-
Skinned strangers whose
Worn undergarments,
Ferried here from
Unremembered Italian
Villages, held the grime
And loss of a new life
Not much better
Than ours. But her voice,
Honeyed by the sweet
Black Southern earth,
Which she'd forsaken
For new love and another

New beginning, clutched
Within it a divine
Light so impossibly rich
It rendered my music-
Wild daydreams delicious,
Pure enough to pursue
Like God Himself in
The dreadful crush of days
After the crashing
Suddenness of her death.

Now, after eons of
Starlit darkness west
Of New York, as we bend
Up along the sweep of
This city's golden coast,
Feeling in the sway
Of this steel body
The winds shoving across
Lake Michigan, I feel
A warm cleansing
Trepidation of the new,
Just as Mother must have
Felt coming North
To see with a child's
Eyes the perfect beauty
Of her Blackness
As it unfolded against
A freshly painted sky.

Longingly I see her now –
A holy radiance glowing
Above the big-shouldered
Metropolis where,
Tomorrow night, against

The shimmering rush
Of Rush Street, I will sing
her back to life, and,
In the crystalline
Stillness of Mister Kelly's,
Climb up to her in heaven
On the silver rungs
Of her favorite songs.

POEMS OF ARAB ANDALUSIA

Turtles cavort

in their capes of green algae.

– Ibn Sarah

I.

In one of these poems, the poet
writes, 'Birds trill on the branches
like singing girls / bending
over their lutes', and when I look up,
I see them outside my window,
on this last warm day of winter,
looking not lost but adrift.

'She is an immigrant', I read,
'from other lands'.

On the table beside me, a teapot
of steaming water, a sachet of Ceylon,
a teddy bear of honey. My father
in the curling steam. 'Inside
the palanquins on the camels' backs
I saw their faces beautiful
as moons / behind veils
of gold cloth'. Tell me, Friend,
who is it who worries so much
about the turtles, wrapped in ribbons
of foam, lounging on the lonely
beaches of Andalusia?

II.

Once a student asked you
if it mattered, all this effort
and pain, losing sleep, your health,
all the loneliness it entailed,
to puzzle through the words of
dead poets. That night, you,
a young man too, opened up
this anthology, a gift from
a friend long forgotten, and found
the answer:

> *Look at me,*
> *I dress myself in the white*
> *of white hair*
> *in mourning for youth.*

Your pillow in the morning
was a turtle swimming in a sea
of tears, carrying another
load of words. What hatched
within the sand: the vocabulary
of wholeness taken slow.

III.

as the light of wakefulness

                                         fills the body

as the whir of holiness

                                         tunes the soul

as the aftermath of heartbreak

                                         thimbles gratitude

into each passing hour

as the sweep of time

nuzzles its hot breath

against the embers

of a lived life

against *spheres*

of dalliance

and pleasure

IV.

Remembering: one evening, after school:
a peaceful blizzard: the chime-heavy
ruefulness of snow falling in great big clumps:
the parking lot: a snowball fight: the snowballs
arcing through the pink sky: the snowballs
bursting open mid-flight: the snowballs
like shooting stars: the wishes
wished: the innocence of boyhood
reawakened: the perfection of it: the rest
of your life as untouched: then the morning,
years later, as you drove to school,
reminded of that evening by the white snow
of spring blossoms: how deeply you wept,
remembering that evening, the snow:
the warmth, the companionship, the unutterable
thing that waits on the other side of retirement:
the mathematics of clocks: the mathematics
of memory: the mercy of remembering,
of snowballs returning to snow.

V.

A book set on fire
provides a different kind
of warmth.

Our winged mothers taught us
to love ourselves. We are obedient
children. We are honest.

'She may not know
where the mosque is', I read, 'but she knows
the location / of all the taverns'.

Our hands hold the words
of dead poets. Time holds as still
as turtles asleep in the trees.

VI.

as the ghosts arrive along the shore

        to sing their songs

    to the sea

            as we go from lost

     to adrift

VII.

The tea has gone cold.
The student is somewhere else,
surprised by the depths
of his sadness.
Perhaps he now understands
this craving for poems.

Snow, even in June.
Snow, dusting every memory of Andalusia.

Our mothers, our fathers,
their voices
humming forever in the latticed history
of our bones.

Evening arrives, too soon.

The tree, again
a collection of vacancies.

The silences, nothings
readying for the next poem.

Let us turn the page together
and read: 'There are splendors of such perfection
they all bring to mind

the beauty of absolute certainty,
the radiance of faith'.

VIII.

as we go from lost

          to adrift

               to dust

     may it be

       with the urgency

      of turtles

IV

MIGRATION NARRATIVE

What wilts becomes
the world for the weary.
They can't help but

wonder at the lovely
shadow touch of another
war's rubbled song.

If crossing freely into fire
can churn the blood's
hollow music, then

surely the orphan can
ask at dusk for water
and get more than spit.

AUTOBIOGRAPHY

It will include   a photograph   black-and-white –
my father   young   dapper   dark
three-piece suit   glum-eyed   leaning
against the hurt-   braided trunk   of a banyan tree
a peony   white flame of heartbreak   held
within his trembling   hand   an offering
to dull the edges   of a loneliness   deeper
than longing   than blood   than grief   a Chinese girl
fiancée stolen   by death   a young heart
vanquished   the wedding diamond   hurled
into   the foamy anguish   of the South China Sea
it is 1968   ten years   after   his
father's death   ten years   before
my arrival   between   the two fatherhoods
hands holding together   his splintered   goodness
the delirium   this garden   Hong Kong   the sea
a black ribbon slicing across   the trembling backdrop
this April   afternoon   sunlight   glinting
misty air   Pakistan   the light   in the wake
of Partition   more dream   than memory
to imagine   what sufferings   lie huddled
like orphans   in his heart   is to imagine
the unfinished   story   of every son's love
for his father   is to knit a blanket   of wind   with horizon
thread   to wrap oneself   in its dissolving
light   is to sit down   with a pencil
promising   to begin   the next letter home   with
yet   or   *and*   with the prayers
keepsaked   within those   tiny words   is to look
into   the crumpled   pages   of the peony's
bursting   white body   and see   lurking

within it   another love   waiting   its turn
        to surge   into this story   I want to call
    out   from a future   too impossible
to invent   from a time   before   my father
    joined his father   in the earth   to say   Father
        do not   look upon   the churning   waters
    of the bay with such   hungry pain   do not wonder
with such restless eyes   about   the easy lives
    of fish   instead   Father   walk backwards
        to your apartment   fix yourself   some tea
    and as you   pluck free each   large petal
of the flower   searching for   its inner sun
    let the warm taste   of home   bring to mind
        the life-saving   possibility

                        of me

WHAT THE WIND SAID TO ME WHEN I AWOKE FROM ANOTHER NIGHTMARE IN WHICH MY FATHER HAD DIED, ALONE

I was there with him in the darkness
of your dream, was his breath, was the frayed
scarf of it, the shivering white dust of it,

was the moist cobweb across his mouth,
was the last vapor of life curled into a whistled
sound, a word repeated – something like *face*
and *soul*, or *fast* and *silly*, like *fist* hitting
soil, like *fish* thrashing in the jaws of *seal* –
a name, a name. *Yours.* You

should have been there too, with me,
strumming the black etchings of his face, his palms,
letting your fingertips quell the scorch of skin,
freeing me to braid my howling immateriality
into the thready blare of the trumpet,
to become the bridge between worlds,
become the emblazoned quiver of horizon
as the sun rises to no chorus.

★

In the village, where I found
your father
lying in bed, his head turned toward Mecca,
his hands folded across his belly,
posing already
for the grave. He said *sing*.
But the songbird beneath his window refused.
Silence reigned, broken by rain,

the rumble of electric sky.
The future's grim shadow cast itself into the dream,
falling across his body like the gnarled limb
of an ancient tree.

Other winds blew. Rain, so much rain.

★

Perhaps, then, it was pity
which moved me to kiss his forehead
and massage away
the swelling of his splintered feet,
wail sweetly in his ears
to keep the crush of songlessness at bay
as the waters rose around him —

to pretend that I was you
as the current tore him away from this world,
from me.

★

Without you, songbird: woodswallow, magpie
bulbul, goldfinch, oriole, crow,
whatever —

without his oldest, the only child privy
to the torture of his secret griefs,
the way his kin stole the most delicious pulp of his life,
leaving only the rinds,
as glorious and golden as rinds can be,

the way he offered up even these
nothings

when they came back and he had no more to give,
leaving his children,
their mother,
wondering at their own share,

the way he loved most the ones who caused him
the most suffering,

alone,
he bit his lip until the taste of blood
reminded him
of your absence, because you had wounded him
by demanding he be a father,
nothing else.

He hated that you took pride
in your violence.

★

When he asked me, the wind, what my name was,
I gave yours.
What right did I have to deny
a dying man's wish
when to fulfill it would give me, the nothingness
that I am, a father?

By now blind, he believed I was you
when I folded myself at his feet,
called him *Daddy*, and wept
as I expanded like a tempest to fill the room,
to obliterate the world, as only a man's son can.

Then he smiled, knowingly, saying into me,
as he passed on,

      Yes,

            yes,

                  yes

                                      – to what,
I cannot say, but perhaps you,
awake now, with your ill father still
alive, and material,
already know the answer, and perhaps
you can mouth it in song or sigh,
in prayer or embrace, in *caw*
or *coo*.

                 ★

I am,
if not you, then your dearest friend,
your brother, burning
to carry your voice, your supplication,
every note and knot of it,
down this mountain,
across the flooded valley,
through fields of wheat and corn,
through an endless pummel
of rain, across the great plains
of silence and time, beyond the shores
of language, beyond the void
from which every wind is born, some as sighs,
some as swells, as storms,
as silence.

I am
a wind born of such silence, and that man
with empty hands,
he is my father now.

Whatever you can give,
while you still have time left
in which to give,
give.

TO BE A FISHERMAN, OR A FATHER, YOU MUST

Observe the wonders as they occur around you.
Do not claim them. Feel the artistry
moving through, and be silent.
– from 'Body Intelligence', Rumi

Know that inside the glistening bodies of fish, within secret
Envelopes wonder compels us to tear open, there lie, like ore,
Vast stretches of empty hours, mined from our lives, time
Invested in the pursuit of mere existence, of letting our own
Natural radiance loose, and nothing more, and nothing less.

And so you float upon the heavens-heavy surface of the water,
Looking at neither side of the reflection, but rather at your own
Inner burning, from which a new kind of love is being forged.

Like starlight, having traversed centuries to catch your son's
Attention while he studies his own window of night, your soul,
Keeping time with breath, also travels between the living
And the lost, between life's riddles and its blessings. You see,
Nothing depends on the catch. Rather, true wisdom is rooted
In casting yourself into the growing grandeur of this new love.

ZINNIAS. HOW. FOREVERNESS.

Zinnias, dahlias, peonies all pluck from the sweet
air of these faraway spring days another breathless
yearning for warmer things. We dream of golden
angles of sun, silver scribbles of rain, the thronging
noisome earth waking again in soggy greenness.

How is it, then, that despite this longing, we find
inside each waking moment a blissful stillness
nuanced by frolic and coo? This bright, beautiful boy
anchors every goodness, his wonder gracing ours.

Foreverness is the only way to measure love, is
another wisdom he gifts, is a daily bread to give life
its blazing awe. So we set ourselves awhirl in joy,
sing fire into this slow, snow-filled February,
and let his enchanted ways wrap our hearts with
light, three buds readying to burst into music.

TO A SON ABOUT TO GIVE HIS FATHER A KIDNEY

– for AC and DC

I.

I need to think beyond his illness,
beyond the gathering weight
of uncertainty and see – instead of
the red blur of my mother's roses
browning beside his bed – his living
eyes, the charred edges of each
passing hour, my own bronze fingers
opening and closing around his
every puff of breath, a rehearsal
of sorts for when this now has passed
like light beyond the graspable.

Until then, mouthfuls of mud.
But also the buoyant scent
of freshly baked bread in the oven,
his face waiting to be found
in every window, the book of bedtime
stories always under my bed.

II.

It has been years since I turned
to God for answers.

Tonight, alone in his house,
nearly destroyed by the heart-rending

pleasure of Mozart's *Requiem*,
I pull from the bookshelf
a Bible, see a playing card borrowed
from his box of magic tricks
marking a page in the Book of Psalms.
I begin to read, addressing
whatever spirits lurk in the shadows:

*Even the darkness is not dark
to You, and the night is as bright
as the day. Darkness and light
are alike to You. For You
formed my inward parts; You wove me
in my mother's womb. I will give
thanks to You, for I am fearfully
and wonderfully made; wonderful
are Your works, and my soul
knows it well.*

III.

  When inside the body a window
opens, and from that window
   steps forth another window,
which opens for another opening
   window until it is impossible
to keep count of windows,
  of endless openings –
     then it is time.

IV.

We sit on opposite sides of a booth,
beside the window, an untouched
basket of warm bread between us,
stirring sugar into our mugs,
this pancake house how we return
to each other every Sunday,
the divorce old news now, the distance
of it growing smaller each year,
the rest of our lives growing
smaller, too. I taste the wet earth
in my mouth, try to swallow it away,
wash it clean with each slow sip.

I ask my father if the pain
still keeps him awake at night.
With a smiling wink, a quick glance past me,
he tells me it gives him more time
to think about me, that suffering
is what separates us from
other kinds of living beings,
that God made us in His own image,
that no doubt sometimes
He too suffers seated upon
His throne in heaven, finds it hard
to sleep, is grateful to have
more time to worry about
the world He created.

By the time our server delivers our eggs,
refills our coffee, our conversation
has found its way to baseball,
to Opening Day, to the Cubs, to how

it would forever break his heart
that his father, God rest his soul,
didn't live long enough to see
his Lovable Losers finally win it all.

When he lets me pay the bill,
I understand that in my blood,
the decision, which no one wanted
me to make, has already been made.

V.

Even the half-moon
          provides light enough
                    to read the names
          etched in stone,
the names of those
          who came before you,
                    who made the world
          the world for you.
And whatever
          your eyes cannot decipher,
                    let your fingers trace.

VI.

I touch the places on my body
beneath which are buried
two kingdoms that, if I am to believe
the Chinese herbalist I spoke to
last week in search of other
wisdoms, belong more

to our ancestors and our offspring
than to us. Later, on the car ride home,
my mother, speaking in her usual
poetry, says, after I refused
to reconsider as my father had
begged me to do: 'Then, son,
if you must go ahead with this, then
do not think of it as giving.
Rather, as a way of returning
inherited riches'.

When she wipes away tears,
I understand that it is part of her
body that I would be losing,
that, despite the world they had built
between them, I am living proof
of the love they once shared,
and still do in a darkness
made of light – a love
both wonderful and fearful,
mine to hold, mine to pass on,
mine to return.

THE BREATH INSIDE THE BREATH

Listen, my friend. He who loves understands.
– Kabir

So it happens: walking with soul wide open toward the rising sun,

    A man, as if shot, goes still, his breath suddenly caught by some

Cosmic hook slung down from the heavens. He collapses, knees to earth,

    Hand clutched to heart, and asks the Almighty, in gasps of silence, for

Instructions on surviving this panic. The answer, a tangle of sound,

    Nudged along on a remembering wind, arrives as a blessing, a name

Blooming as new life upon his lips, as breath inside breath. The man,

    Plucked from the pinch of death, rises up on wings of gratitude,

And sings, first of God, then of a friend – of *him* – turns then to face

    The sun, brighter now, a mirror. There, in the healing awe of light,

Edged in gold, sits a tuning fork, iron hot, ready to be struck again.

    Lifed by love, he listens to the music of a shared cosmos, cries,

Ameen, ameen, ameen.

THE WOODEN BALCONIES OF OLD LAHORE

– For Tasneem Raja

When it begins to rain on this summer night,
I step out onto the balcony to watch with nostalgia
the shirtless boys of our mohalla thrash about
in the flooded plaza below. Down each one
of the three narrow streets that all arrive at this triangular
juncture hang balconies carved of wood by hands
that lived in the century before the last, each enchanted
structure a small portal to the past. The fantastic
imaginations of the families who commissioned their ornate
designs still on display. Some showcase a geometric
intricacy on par with the inner trellises of the human brain;
others bear the likenesses of bears emerging
from massive Ottoman tulips, camels crossing sand-dunes
shaped like ocean waves. Even cat-eyed serpents
swallowing their own tails, as if predicting
the floundering tomorrows of our fought-for nation.
Our balcony, seemingly conceived during a monsoon
like tonight's, quite possibly by someone seeing the same
splashing scene of playfulness that I am seeing
from above, depicts a series of mermaids swimming
through coils of seaweed, each reaching to a
mirrored twin, seeking rescue. I see I am not alone,
that others have come out to delight in the rain rinsing away
the dust and longing of another brutal day spent seeking respite
in shade. Even the unmarried daughters of the old
Haji Ali Samdani look on with lusting
eyes, peeking from dark scarves to see their future
husbands frolicking beneath the falling sky,
measuring the wildness of each prospective lover to guess
at the lastingness of his goodness. Everything seems

more perfect, more everlasting, during the rainy season,
when instead of noticing the slow but inevitable
decay of wooden things, or the dimming
vitality of our aging bodies, we feel suddenly young
again, held intact within the timelessness of these miniature
museums whose magic will inevitably end
in collapse, in the kind of crushing stillness that follows
the last drop of rain, the last silent grasp of breath.

ARCHEOLOGY

In silent self-mourning, we gathered
one last time, suspended in the amber
of our moon, then spent our final days

in a cave, praying for forgiveness as
we carved with flint shard the histories
of our tribes into the colossal bones

of creatures now extinct, aware, through
the blinding labor of each recorded
name, of our own impending doom

at the hands of invading cousins who
knew nothing of memory, nor cared to
remember. Departure, this time, would

occur not in body, but in the body's
blood, in the spilling of the distilled
moonlight we had begun to keepsake

within it since we first saw the signs
in the weeping faces of our children,
in the sparking panic of stars unmoored

from night. When, millennia later,
the stones we died holding, buried
beneath volumes of stone and steel, are

unearthed, then conferred with story, we
wonder if they will be called weapons,
if each chapter of our existence, etched

into reassembled monsters, will reveal
an undying taste for torture and destruction,
        if the blame for our demise will be

our crown to wear until no one remains
        to hold it. Mostly, when we lie deep within
the humming belly of the earth, awaiting

        excavation, we will wonder if any of our
inner light will remain, if the living will still have
        eyes human enough to see it.

BLOOD HARMONIES

To remember my mother crouching in our kitchen,
putting into place a new floor of ceramic tiles,
is to remember her blood hopes, her effervescent hunger
to keep the feet of her five kids from slipping
into the wrong kind of slide. Stay one with one another,
in blood harmony, she would say, meaning
brother and sister, Muslim and Muslim, blood and blood.
Pointing down at the tiles, she would say,
Look how the pattern comes together,
forms a larger mosaic of meaning. You should live like this.
Most of the time, I nodded my head, not knowing
how else to respond, agreeing because it was simpler.
But sometimes, standing there, looking down
at a floor not yet finished, at naked patches revealing
a history of vinyl, broken and stained, I would think,
I just can't be happy living so small, so safe.
Then I would see, in those unfinished places, the face
of some girl I had met the other day,
whose name I never asked, knowing it was pointless.
I would stand there in the kitchen, thinking
how badly I wanted to know that girl's name, to believe in it
like a new religion, like my own blood,
how I wanted to let myself fall in love with her,
because that girl had smiled at me, because that girl was real
and alive, not like one of those phantom wives
my mother saw in her dreams and spoke of in metaphors.

THE TOMORROWS

My mother   born a decade   after Partition,
   grew up in a whisper-   haunted era
of self-induced   healing   she had no way
   of understanding   seeing her mother's eyes
go still in the midst   of a story   long enough
   for some unspeakable   hurt to creep
across her face   like a translucent   spider
   she recognized   the treachery   of grief
sharpened   by being alive   never asked
   about migration –   about brothers'   song-
choked throats   knifed   for knowing
   the Ninety-Nine Names   of God   or not
about sisters   already drowned   by misery
   deflowered   by dacoits   whose pockets
had no more space   for gold   for spoils
   then dropped   by their families
into wells to safeguard   the purity   of their own names –
   survival   be it miracle   or mirage
depended upon   a total annihilation
   of the lost   whose incomplete   ghosts
appeared during moments   of stillness   their still-
   kicking hearts   held out   offerings
to the living   begging them   with blighted eyes
   to forever hold fast   to silence   or if
when their children came   bloated
   with curiosity   waving   their own
daggers   to speak to them   only of
   the untarnished majesty   of their
             tomorrows

THE RIDDLE OF LONGING

When to be an immigrant's
son is to be a speaker of several

broken tongues, each day
leaves you homesick

for a place you've never
touched, nor forgotten, and feel

the ache to know. When there is
no one left, you ask the wind

for directions. Your own
voice returns with a map

of your mother's palms spoken
into threads of tangled blue

light. Take the long way
home, through the cemetery.

There, kiss your father's name,
bring back an echo of grief,

and a phlox. When years
later your son finds it crushed

within a book, he will feel
against his face a warm puff

of your living breath, then
a wink of green wings behind

his eyes. Strange, that I am
holding two large rocks,

looking for something else
sacred to smash open.

GHAZAL FOR THE LOST

None of the unspeaking souls on this morning train knows where we are going.
Waking again to a washed-clean darkness, we prefer the frightening disquiet of mystery.

To bear witness to the disappearing bravery of the night's last remaining star
Is to walk alone through the hills without water, is to fill your mouth with mystery.

Inside each bird in the taxidermist's house, hidden between folds of crumpled paper –
The photograph of a child, bright eyes of a surrogate heart, their youthful mystery.

Why must every breath come at a cost? Each passing minute steal from us the color
And strength of our bodies? To live is to be a dying thing, all else is mystery.

Prayer directs our longing toward Mecca, keeps our foreheads anchored to the earth.
Each step is touched by language, but between prostrations: silence, and mystery.

When the rain begins to fall, sending shivers of joy through the dead desert air,
A sleeping dog lifts his head from the sand, watches the washing away of mystery.

As you arrive at your final destination, a village carved from a mountain's hip,
A castle at its center, drop your body, begin to climb, be no longer afraid of mystery.

Do you remember, Faisal, what the elders preached about forgetting? Centuries of grief
Had made them wise, taught them to seek the mercy and goodness of mystery.

ABOUT THE AUTHOR

I ask the lion lurking beyond the irascible tempt of longing

        to open his mouth and come closer, closer. I put my head

inside his jaws, feel the moist smite of hot breath against

        my cheeks, catch a shiver of antelope blood on my tongue.

I call him King, ask if he prefers a different name, if

        the unspeakable loneliness of kings ever makes him wish

he lived elsewhere, perhaps in a luxury loft in some sprawling city,

        had an office job that paid a touch too well, could ride

a train to and from work, nurse a planter of grass on his balcony

        and sweet-dream it into the Serengeti whenever he felt

a pang of homesickness blooming in his gut. I turn to look down

        his throat, expecting to see a pink fleshy cave of

hunger. Instead, I find a round window revealing the peppery

        blackness of night, a host of giddy stars shooting

through the vastness. I forget my life is hovering on the wild

        edge of slaughter, then remember. I close my eyes,

expecting each passing second to be my last, for the lion's teeth

        to tear into my face, crush my skull like a cantaloupe.

I wait until I become a part of him, until the sky cowers into itself,

        swallowing me like a tooth. Soon I sense him crying,

a child's soft, voiceless sobbing, a song. I open my eyes, see

        I'm wearing a watch, sitting alone on a park bench in the dying

orange of evening, feeding stale bread to a posse of pigeons,

        while above me an airplane crashes into the sun.

A CLOSING

SONG OF MYSELF AS A TOMORROW

It is not far — it is within reach;
Perhaps you have been on it since you were born, and did not know;
Perhaps it is everywhere, on water and on land.
— from 'Song of Myself', Walt Whitman

In America — where my face is anything
but American, I lunge for self-annihilation whenever
another set of monstering eyes double-barrels me

                             enemy
        outsider
                sandnigger
                                 terrorist
        murderer   thief
           target practice
                     less-than
dog   shitface   trespasser
                   imposter
        invader
                camel jockey
                       terrorist   *Muslim*
        abuser
           enemy   foreigner
                  disembodied
           Bedouin

But erasure —
what can it do when the blood's trajectory
has forever been about becoming another river, about winding its way
along some other pathway toward survival? How else
could I have come to be when

                    pillage

                                                loss
        civil war   Partition
                    loss
        displacement

                        Partition   loss
                                    silence

            Partition
loss

                        migration

                                            heartache

            grief

                            separation
                    loss

                                                displacement
            Partition
                    displacement   silence
migration   loss
                        Partition
            Partition

                                        displacement
                        silence
                hunger

        touched every moment
        of my parents' lives
        cobbled together

        onto the unlived tomorrows of children?
        To plunge into tomorrow requires the existence
        of a tomorrow to plunge into –

I am that tomorrow, lost within the land
beyond where all rivers end,

in the barren vastness of an untethered
darkness where survival means

remembering my parents' tomorrows,
knifing new furrows through which their refugee blood
can flow –
means saying, despite the price
of standing tall and free,

        Yes

                to exile

           Yes

      to America

NOTES

Pakistan, Fatherless: Iqbal is Sir Muhammad Iqbal (1877-1938), often referred to as Allama Iqbal, the great Indian poet-philosopher who is considered, along with Muhammad Ali Jinnah (1876-1948), one of the founders of the nation of Pakistan. Even though he did not live to see independence, his ideas and writing helped propel the movement to establish a separate majority Muslim state. His 'Taranah-e-Hindi', published in 1904, is partly a love song to India, partly an anthem protesting the rule of the British Raj. The epigraph for this book is excerpted from this piece; many thanks to Zafar Malik for help with the translation.

Faisalabad: The third most populous city in Pakistan, it was called Lyallpur (for Sir James Broadwood Lyall) until 1977 when it was renamed after the late King Faisal of Saudi Arabia.

Bhagat Singh: Considered a national hero and martyr in both India and Pakistan, Singh (1907-1931) was a revolutionary freedom fighter, born in Lyallpur, who was executed by hanging after being convicted of murdering an English police officer. An epic hunger strike while in prison helped him become a household name. Even though he and Gandhi remained at odds due to Singh's willingness to resort to violence whenever necessary, it is said that Jawaharlal Nehru and Muhammad Ali Jinnah each visited Singh during his hunger strike, and each commended the man's devotion toward the cause of independence. Their praise helped solidify his legendary status.

Denaturalization: An Elegy for Mr Vaishno Das Bagai, an American: Vaishno Das Bagai (1891-1928) immigrated to San Francisco from Peshawar, now in Pakistan, in 1915, in order to escape British colonial rule, more freely participate in the efforts of the

Gadar Party as it promoted Indian independence, and enjoy the seemingly limitless promise of America. He established himself as a successful businessman and strove to assimilate into American culture. In 1920, after severing all ties to Great Britain, he became a naturalized U.S. citizen. However, following the landmark 1923 Supreme Court case *United States v. Bhagat Singh Thind*, which revoked the citizenship of 'all Asiatics', dozens of naturalized Indian Americans, including Bagai, became 'nationless'. Unable to return to India, and unable to deal with this devastating blow, especially in the midst of the rampant anti-Asian discrimination in the 1920s, Bagai committed suicide in 1928 as an act of protest. He left behind notes for his wife and three sons, and penned an additional letter, which was sent to, and subsequently published in, the *San Francisco Examiner*. The epigraph of this poem is excerpted from the *Examiner*. In the fourth section of the poem, the two questions as well as the italicized lines are taken directly from the Supreme Court ruling. The Rani Bagai epigraph is from *Bridges Burnt Behind: The Story of Vaishno Das Bagai*, courtesy of the Angel Island Immigration Station Foundation (www.aiisf. org). Many thanks to Judy Yung and Erika Lee whose book *Angel Island: Immigrant Gateway to America* (Oxford University Press, 2010) opened the door to this poem. Thanks also to the South Asian American Digital Archive (www.saada.org) for helping me more fully imagine a way through that door.

In Defense of Monsters: During the coverage of the March 22, 2017, terrorist attack on Westminster Bridge in London, England, where a man, a self-identified Muslim Briton, killed four people and injured more than fifty by crashing into them with his car, a photograph of an unidentified hijab-wearing Muslim woman walking past a victim while on her cell phone went viral. Many people on social media referred to the woman as a 'monster', interpreting her attention to her phone as further evidence that Muslims support terrorism, practice a heartless religion, and feel, at best, indifferent to the carnage perpetrated in 'the name of' their/ our religion. The epigraph is excerpted from the woman's response to this inflammatory coverage.

The Salvation of _Aurella Aurita_: Inspired by a NASA study on microgravity, whose lead scientist was Dorothy Spangenberg, a research professor in the pathology department at Eastern Virginia Medical School.

What Awaits is Made More Luminous By the Blooming Light of Youth: For all students (especially my own) as they hurtle towards graduation; and to those students (especially my own) who have already graduated. No educator teaches alone, even when he feels alone; thus, the poem, an acrostic, spells out, 'Best Wishes from _Us_'.

Poems of Arab Andalusia: All the quoted lines, those in italics, and the epigraph from Ibn Sarah, are taken from the anthology _Poems of Arab Andalusia_ – translated by Cola Franzen and published by City Lights Books (1990) – after which the poem is titled.

The following poems are acrostics:
'Pakistan, Fatherless'
'The Faces of the Holy'
'Remembering Stella and Lily, Who Died on the
        Same Day'
'What Awaits is Made More Luminous By the Blooming
        Light of Youth'
'To Be a Fisherman, or a Father, You Must'
'Zinnias. How. Foreverness.'
'The Breath Inside the Breath'

ACKNOWLEDGEMENTS

My deepest thanks to the editors and staff of the following publications where many of these poems first appeared, sometimes in different forms:

Atlanta Review 'Ayodhya'
Catamaran Literary Reader 'The Wooden Balconies of
        Old Lahore'
Chicago Quarterly Review 'Being in Touch', 'Lost Earring',
        'Zinnias. How. Foreverness.'
Fifth Wednesday Journal Plus 'My Mother's Darkness'
Glass: A Journal of Poetry 'Ghazal for the Lost'
HazMat Review   'Advice to Religious Fanatics'
the minnesota review 'The Salvation of *Aurella Aurita*'
Narrative 'Bhagat Singh', 'Denaturalization: An Elegy
        for Mr Vaishno Das Bagai, an American',
        'Faisalabad'
The *Missouri Review* 'The Opening'
Painted Bride Quarterly 'The Riddle of Longing'
Papercuts 'Ghazal for the Diaspora'
Poet Lore 'Blood Harmonies', 'Song'
Prairie Schooner 'Migration Narrative', 'Poems of Arab
        Andalusia', 'What the Wind Said to Me When
        I Awoke from Another Nightmare in which
        My Father had Died, Alone'
Quiddity 'Archaeology', 'To a Son About to Give His
        Father a Kidney'
RHINO 'Of the Punjab', 'Partition, and Then',
        'Whenever He Teaches *Hamlet*'
The Rumpus 'On the Morning of November 9, 2016,
        I had an Entire Pumpkin Pie for Breakfast',
        'Remembering Stella and Lily, Who Died on the
        Same Day', 'To Be a Fisherman, or a Father, You Must'

Tinderbox Poetry Journal 'About the Author'
wildness 'Autobiography'
'Afterwards' appeared in *The Book of Donuts* (Terrapin Books, 2017), edited by Jason Lee Brown and Shanie Latham.

'Ayodhya' and 'Blood Harmonies' also appeared in *Indivisible: An Anthology of Contemporary South Asian American Poetry* (University of Arkansas Press, 2010), edited by Neelanjana Banerjee, Summi Kaipa, and Pireeni Sundaralingam.

'Ella Fitzgerald, Entering Chicago by Train, Remembers Her Mother's Voice' won Second Place in the 2017 Gwendolyn Brooks Poetry Competition sponsored by the Illinois State Library and the Illinois Center for the Book; a recording of the poem is featured on the website of Kevin Stein, Poet Laureate of the State of Illinois.

'Song of Myself as a Tomorrow' appeared in the anthology *Misrepresented People: Poetic Responses to Trump's America* (New York Quarterly Books, 2018), edited by María Isabel Alvarez and Dante Di Stefano.

Some of the poems in this collection appeared in the chapbook *The Riddle of Longing*, published by Backbone Press in 2017. Gratitude to Crystal Simone-Smith and everyone at Backbone.

Gratitude to my parents – Rahat Mohyuddin and the late Mohammad Mohyuddin – for enduring the hardships of migration, separation, and self-sacrifice in order to provide me and my siblings with lives blessed with love, safety, taqwa, cultural pride, education, opportunity, compassion, and humility. To my siblings – Aisha, Tahir, Rabiya, and Adil – for having been such an integral and necessary part of this journey. To my parents-in-law, Hawa Sodha and the late Esmail Sodha, as well as the entire Sodha family, for their love, kindness, and support. To my extended family in the United States, Pakistan, Great Britain, Canada, India, wherever else they may be – be they living or dead, known or unknown.

Thank you to my dearest friends, mentors, teachers, and fellow writers whose support, love, and guidance have been integral to my growth as a person and poet: Sachin Patel, Ariel Tesher, Shervon Cassim, Alfonso Li, Kevin Lakani, Paul Lusson, Paul Swanson, Lindsey Choy, Ann Cocks, Judi Elman, Eileen McMahon, Tom Koulentes, Liane Fitzgerald, Anne Isaacson, Sue Jamison, Katie Zoloto, Yasmin Saikia, Chad Haines, Cherif Keita, Maimouna Toure-Keita, Wasif Latif, Tasneem Raja, Nisar Naseeruddin, Beth Prusiecki, Samantha Kennedy, Harry Williams, Mark Unno, Mamadou Moustapha Fall, Sadia Uqaili, Nabeela Rasheed, Julian Ryu, Syed Hazique Mahmood, Adam Stern, Martha Edwards, Tony Romano, Henry Sampson, Kevin Brewner, Casey Pawlak, Shawn Shiflett, Randy Albers, Don De Grazia, Nami Mun, Clare Rossini, Dagny Bloland, Peg Kritzler, Syed Afzal Haider, Jean-Claude Loubières, the late Ron Offen, and the late Helen Degen Cohen.

Gratitude to the poets and friends who offered encouragement and guidance during some of the most critical junctures of the writing process: Zafar Malik, Neelanjana Banerjee, Greg Hewett, Rajiv Mohabir, Shadab Zeest Hashmi, Kaveh Akbar, Anita Olivia Koester, Dilruba Ahmed, Leila Chatti, Raena Shirali, Jacob Zawa, Hari Alluri, Leah Umansky, Ralph Hamilton, Deborah Fleming, Dante Di Stefano, Casey Thayer, Jacob Saenz, Kevin Stein, Li-Young Lee, Kathleen Rooney, Tania Runyan, Janice Moore Fuller, Mariam Gomaa, and Jamal Nasir.

Thank you to my friends, colleagues, and students at Highland Park High School, particularly the supremely talented, dedicated, giving people of the English Department; so much love, reverence, and gratitude for the gifts you have given me for the past 15 years.

Thank you to my Narrative 4 family, especially Colum McCann, Lisa Consiglio, Lee Keylock, Kandice Cole, Karen Hollins, Kelsey Roberts, Charles Miles, and Ron Rash; I remain in awe of the work you/we do.

Thank you to Todd Swift, Rosanna Hildyard, Alex Payne, and the amazing team at Eyewear Publishing for ushering this book into the world with such energy, care, vision, and love. And to Edwin Smet for designing such a beautiful cover and book.

Kimiko Hahn, thank you forever for making all the difference in the world!

Gratitude and love to my son, Zayan, the brightest source of light and joy in my life, the most important person for whom I write. May these poems help illuminate the stories of those who came before you and guide you forward.

And, most emphatically, endless thanks to my brilliant and beautiful wife Hina for her love, companionship, faith, sacrifice, patience, wisdom, guidance, and moral compass. Without her, this book would not exist, the person I am today would not exist. With her in my life, there can be no displacement; with her, I will always know home. I love you.

EYEWEAR PUBLISHING

TITLES INCLUDE